The TINIEST GIANTS

A DOUBLEDAY BOOK FOR YOUNG READERS

The TINIEST GIANTS

DISCOVERING DINOSAUR EGGS

Lowell Dingus and Luis Chiappe

A DOUBLEDAY BOOK FOR YOUNG READERS

Published by
Random House, Inc.
1540 Broadway
New York, New York 10036

Library of Congress Cataloging-in-Publication Data
Dingus, Lowell.
    The tiniest giants: discovering dinosaur eggs / Lowell Dingus, Luis
    Chiappe.
        p. cm.
Summary: Describes the efforts of paleontologists to arrange an
expedition to search for dinosaur fossils in the inhospitable region
of southern South America known as Patagonia.
    ISBN 0-385-32642-4
    1. Dinosaurs —Patagonia (Argentina and Chile) —Juvenile
literature.   [1. Paleontology—Patagonia (Argentina and Chile)
2. Dinosaurs—Patagonia (Argentina and Chile)]   I. Chiappe, Luis M.
II. Title
QE862.D5D49285   1999
567.9′0982′7—dc21   98-28886
                                                                          CIP
                                                                           AC
The text of this book is set in 12.5-point Adobe Garamond.
Book design by Susan Clark Dominguez
Manufactured in the United States of America
June 1999
10 9 8 7 6 5 4 3 2 1

Contents

The Patagonian team who helped make our dreams of discovery come true: Back row (from left to right): Susan Zetkus, Paul Sweet, Marilyn Fox, Osvaldo Dilorio, and Lowell Dingus. Front row (from left to right): Carl Mehling, Javier Guevara, Natalia Klaiselburd, and Pablo Puerta. On ladder: Luis Chiappe. Not shown: Rodolfo Coria, Julia Clarke, Sergio Saldivia, and Sara Bertelli.

One

Dinosaur Dreams

Every paleontologist who studies dinosaurs has a dream. This dream runs through the paleontologist's mind constantly, especially when he or she gets the chance to escape from the office and go out into the field to search for fossils. The dream goes something like this:

You wake up one morning and realize that this day is *the* day—the one you've been looking forward to for many months. Today you're leaving on a trip, but not just any trip. This will be no vacation in the mountains or afternoon at the beach. This will be an expedition in search of buried treasure. But you won't be digging for gold and silver hidden by pirates several hundred years ago. You'll be using all the scientific techniques at your disposal to look for something much, much older—buried bones and other fossil remains of the dinosaurs that ruled Earth more than 65 million years ago. You jump out of bed because you can't wait to get going.

To find the dinosaur fossils, you'll fly to some far-off, exotic land where you've always hoped to travel. This place seems dangerous, with desolate deserts, towering volcanoes, and strange animals you've never encountered before.

But the best thing about this place you're traveling to is that it has thousands of acres of beautiful badlands for you to explore. The sun is hot, and the wind blows huge clouds of dust into your face. But you don't really notice. Your eyes are glued to the ground, searching for fragments of fossil bones emerging from the sand and mud.

Suddenly something on the ground catches your eye. You bend down to examine the partly buried object. Sure enough, it's a fossil—the petrified remains of an animal that lived millions of years before any humans inhabited Earth.

Without picking it up, you glance around to see if you can spy any other fossil fragments nearby. To your amazement, the ground is littered with fossils wherever you look. Adrenaline surges through your body, and your heart begins to beat fast. A few quick steps bring you to another small cluster of fossil fragments poking out of the ground. You've discovered a rich new site for dinosaur fossils—and maybe you'll find a kind of dinosaur fossil no one has seen before.

Unfortunately, most paleontologists wake up at this point and realize that they've only been dreaming. But for a few very lucky scientists, this dream comes true.

Our dream came true in South America in 1997. We were looking for the remains of ancient birds and their close dinosaur relatives that lived near the end of the Age of Large Dinosaurs, about 75 million years ago. However, we didn't find any of the things we were looking for. Instead, we found something even more remarkable and totally unexpected: the tiniest giants.

The badlands of Patagonia, where our dreams of discovery came true.

Two

Dinosaur Detectives

We had to do a lot of detective work before we could even begin our expedition. Where should we go to find dinosaur fossils no one had found before? How would we get there? Once we arrived in a remote area, how would we get food and water? If we found fossils, how would we transport them back to a museum? How would we identify what we found and decide whether it was important and new?

If you want to find new dinosaur fossils no one else has found, you usually have to look where no one else has looked. That's exactly what we decided to do. But we didn't simply close our eyes and stick a pin into a map of the world. We gathered clues about where other paleontologists were finding new kinds of dinosaurs.

Since dinosaur fossils were first discovered and recognized as the remains of ancient animals more than 150 years ago, hundreds of kinds have been found. Dinosaur fossils have now been collected on every continent. And given the thousands of scientific studies that have been written, you might think we already know all there is to know about dinosaurs. But nothing could be further from the truth. Each year new discoveries are reported in newspapers, on television, and in scientific journals. Many of these discoveries have been made in the area of southern South America called Patagonia.

Discovered by Europeans in the early 1500s, Patagonia was called the Island of Giants, even though it's not an island. Some historians have argued that the word *Patagonia* comes from the current meaning of the Spanish word *patagón,* "big foot." As the story goes, the Tehuelche Indians who inhabited the region had large feet. So the Spanish called the land Patagonia.

But it seems far more likely that the name really comes from the great explorer Ferdinand Magellan—the leader of the first expedition to sail around the world. Although Magellan died during the voyage, his crew completed the epic journey. When Magellan first encountered the Tehuelche Indians during his voyage in 1520, he called them Patagoni. He drew this name from a famous tale of chivalry that was popular at the time: the story of Primaleón. In the story, a knight-hero decides to fight a giant named Patagón, who lives on a remote island. Thanks to Magellan, the Patagoni were regarded by people back in Europe as giants. In reality, they were of normal height. By naming this part of the world Patagonia, Magellan was probably just trying to enhance his own image as a courageous explorer and legendary hero—as if being the leader of the first crew to sail around the world weren't enough.

Ferdinand Magellan, hero and explorer, who named Patagonia.

Besides being the home of mythical giants and the Tehuelche Indians, Patagonia is one of the largest and most productive dinosaur graveyards in the world, along with Mongolia, China, and the American West. Patagonia encompasses an enormous region, including Tierra del Fuego at the southern tip of South America. It almost covers the southern end of the continent. With an area of more than 400,000 square miles, Patagonia is nearly half the size of Greenland and larger than the states of Texas and Oklahoma combined. All but the western edge of Patagonia lies within Argentina, east of the high, frigid peaks that form the jagged backbone of the Andes mountain range.

Patagonia gets much more rainfall along its western edge than along its eastern side, since little rain makes it over the Andes to fall on the eastern hills and plains. East of the Andes, Patagonia is mostly a barren, dusty desert, whipped by strong gusts of wind. In this desolate and inhospitable land live the puma, the condor, and the ostrichlike rhea. Under them lie abundant remains of past organisms, because Patagonia is covered by layer upon layer of rocks that entomb the fossils of ancient mammals and even more ancient dinosaurs.

In spite of the best efforts of many Argentine and international teams of paleontologists, most parts of Patagonia are still virtually unexplored for fossils. This is partly because Patagonia is so enormous and partly because it is so desolate. Aside from the highways con-

This map of Argentina shows some of the important places where we visited and worked during our expeditions.

necting major cities, roads are rare and unpaved. Many of these smaller roads were built by oil companies during their explorations for oil and natural gas. In the wake of geological teams searching for oil have come smaller field crews of paleontologists prospecting for fossils. But there are still a lot of places in Patagonia where paleontologists have never searched.

In 1996, at the end of a field season devoted to collecting fossils near the city of San Luis in central Argentina, some members of our field crew undertook a brief exploration of the rock layers exposed around the extinct volcano called Auca Mahuida. This region is in the northwest corner of Patagonia about three hundred miles southwest of San Luis and six hundred miles southwest of Buenos Aires as the crow flies. We made this short, exploratory trip because we knew from geologic maps that there were enormous exposures of rocks in this area that were formed near the end of the Age of Large Dinosaurs. More importantly, these rocks had never been prospected for fossils.

Our 1996 expedition discovered some fossil bones of the giant plant-eating dinosaurs called sauropods, as well as some skeletal fragments of other dinosaurs and creatures that lived with them. We could see that the rocks of this region deserved more attention.

Planning the Expedition

We decided to organize another expedition to the area around Auca Mahuida in 1997. This trip would involve a larger crew of fourteen people, and we would spend much more time there. Our initial goal was to find fossils of ancient birds and the small meat-eating (theropod) dinosaurs that are closely related to them. But we knew that we might also locate the remains of other interesting creatures from the Age of Large Dinosaurs.

We had to work out a number of problems before we could embark on such an ambitious adventure. We had to establish agreements with the governments and the paleontologic institutions in the area where we hoped to work. We needed to find funding to buy tents, cooking equipment, food, collecting tools, and airline tickets, as well as to rent vehicles.

Two people on our field crew took charge of making flight arrangements, buying supplies, and renting vehicles. This was an enormous job. The two had to make detailed lists of supplies and then obtain each item. Some things could be purchased in Argentina, but others had to be bought in New York and shipped to Argentina's capital, Buenos Aires.

In developing the collecting agreements with the local governments and institutions in the Patagonian province of Neuquén, where we wanted to do our work, the help of our fellow paleontologist Rodolfo Coria was essential. Rodolfo is a very successful fossil collector at the Carmen Funes Museum in the Argentine town of Plaza Huincul. He has discovered and studied many new dinosaurs in the rock layers of his province, including one of the largest plant-eating sauropods ever found, *Argentinosaurus,* and one of the largest meat-eating theropods ever discovered, *Gigantosaurus.*

Our agreements allowed us to prospect and collect in the area we were interested in. If we were fortunate enough to find fossils, we could take them out of Argentina and back to New York to clean (or prepare) them and study them. After preparing the fossils and publishing scientific articles about them, we would return the specimens to the Carmen Funes Museum.

With generous grants from the National Geographic Society and the InfoQuest Foundation in California, and after many months of planning, we were finally ready to begin our search for ancient birds and other animals in the remote badlands of Patagonia.

Three

Adventure in Argentina

At the end of October 1997, some crew members flew from New York to Buenos Aires to finish buying supplies and rent a van to carry the gear and team members into the field. The rest of our crew flew down the first week in November. In Buenos Aires we met several students and scientists from universities and museums in Argentina who would also be part of the expedition. After we'd shopped for the final items on our supply list, we were ready to start the fourteen-hour drive from Buenos Aires to Auca Mahuida.

From here on, each member of the team would write about his or her daily activities in a small notebook. These writings are called field notes. Making field notes is a very important responsibility because these notes provide a permanent written record of the trip. Months or years from now, crew members and other scientists will be able to read exactly where our expedition went and what it found. Many famous expeditions, whether searching for new fossils, exploring new regions of the continents, or sailing the seas, have been documented this way and later studied.

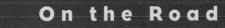

On the Road

November 6. We left Buenos Aires in the afternoon. Our expedition was composed of two vehicles—a pickup truck, which carried most of the field gear, and a van, which carried most of the crew members. For hours we drove through the agricultural heartland of Argentina, a region called La Pampa. The truck and van were running well, which was a relief. It's very frustrating when vehicles break down—then you can't get to the areas where you want to look for fossils. It can also be very expensive to get a van or truck fixed. We stopped about nine in the evening at the small rural town of Pehuajo, about a third of the way to Auca Mahuida. After checking into a

small hotel for the night, we ate dinner at a local restaurant and went to bed. These would be the last beds we would sleep in for about four weeks.

The Puesto

November 7. We drove and drove, hoping to make it all the way to Auca Mahuida by nightfall. The sights along the road taught us a lot about the animals living in Argentina today, especially all the different kinds of birds. It had been an unusually rainy few weeks in La Pampa because of El Niño. Consequently, huge numbers of waterbirds were feeding in the shallow ponds and lakes that had formed along the side of the road. Identifying the flamingos, spoonbills, coots, ducks, and various raptors (birds of prey) kept us alert and amused as the miles rolled by. As we headed further west, the land grew drier and more rugged. We drove along enormous ridges of sand that represented ancient dunes deposited by huge sandstorms near the end of the last ice age, 10,000 to 20,000 years ago.

Juan, an Argentine cowboy, or *gaucho*, lives on the ranch, or *puesto*, where we set up our camp.

Finally, in the late afternoon, we met Rodolfo Coria and his crew members and drove the last sixty miles to our field area as the sun set over the volcano at Auca Mahuida. As darkness descended, we set up our camp at a small ranch. Such small ranches, called *puestos,* are home for rugged ranchers and their families, who raise sheep and goats. This particular *puesto* was owned and managed by Doña Dora, a tough but friendly seventy-year-old native of this region, and her partner, Don José. Along with Doña Dora's grandson, Josecito, and a young Argentine cowboy, or *gaucho*, named Juan, the partners cared for several hundred goats and sheep. Their hospitality and good company were essential to the success of our expedition.

We would occasionally buy one of their goats or sheep for a barbecue called an *asado.* These occasions often turned into parties with Doña Dora and her family. While we ate, we would tell stories about other places we had visited to collect fossils, and they would tell us stories about their *puesto.* The evenings were spectacular, with crimson sunsets followed by starlit skies accented with occasional meteors and passing satellites. The stars in the night sky of Argentina are very different from the ones most of us are used to seeing in the Northern Hemisphere. The Big Dipper and the North Star are not visible from the Southern Hemisphere. Instead we saw the picturesque Southern Cross.

Most nights were cool but not cold—good sleeping weather. (During the day the temperatures stayed in the eighties—not too hot.) Each of us had his or her own tent to crawl into.

Occasionally, if we didn't keep the tents zipped up, local inhabitants like tarantulas would pass through, not to mention the geese, chickens, and dogs that owned our backyard camp.

The *puesto* had no running water, so there were no toilets or showers. The bathroom was behind some distant bush or rocky outcrop, and we washed in the small stream that was still barely running in the riverbed below the *puesto*. We didn't drink the water from it, however. Every few days a couple of crew members would drive back into the city of Neuquén, the capital of the province, to buy groceries and fill our water containers. Cities like Neuquén, which has a population of almost 500,000 people, have all the conveniences of home, including gas stations, laundries, and a supermarket that covers a whole city block. We were quite content and ready for the real adventure to begin.

The Hunt Begins

November 8. After a good night's sleep, we woke up full of excitement. Today, at long

These outcrops behind the *puesto* clearly show the layering that helps scientists figure out how old the rocks are.

last, we could begin prospecting for fossils in the ancient layers of rock that formed the gorgeous cliffs behind the *puesto*. Looking for fossils usually involves a lot more walking than digging. There are two basic kinds of fossil collecting—prospecting and quarrying. When you first begin searching for fossils in a new area, as we were doing, you start by prospecting. You have to search for clues that hint at where a fossilized dinosaur skeleton might be buried. Prospecting involves walking over promising ridges, flats, and ravines while looking for small fragments of fossil bone sticking

Working in the field is dusty and dirty and requires patience, since most of the digging is done by hand. Here Marilyn Fox prepares to apply a protective jacket of plaster bandages around some fossil eggs.

out of the rock layers on the surface of the ground. Whole days can be spent prospecting for fossils without ever digging out a single specimen. While we prospected, we were serenaded by the screeches and squawks of cliff-dwelling parrots.

If you do find the fragmentary clues that lead you to a good fossil, you need to dig it out and take it back to the museum for study. The process of excavating a fossil is called quarrying. It usually involves digging around a bone or skeleton that's buried near the surface of the ground and encasing it in a protective jacket of plaster bandages. Once the bandages dry, the jacket can be lifted out of the ground and transported back to a museum without damaging the fossils inside.

Our first day in the field was not very successful. Mostly we found scraps of fossil bone: some fragments of fossil turtle shell, small pieces of shell from a dinosaur egg, and armor plates from ancient crocodiles. Rodolfo and his crew found the tail section of a small sauropod belonging to the titanosaurs. But it

Sometimes we have to leave fossils in the ground because we don't have time to dig them out. That's what happened with this titanosaur tail being exposed by Sergio Saldivia.

wasn't worth digging up because it would take a lot of time and he already had several similar specimens in his museum. All in all, our first day's results were nothing to write home about.

Judging by the clues in the rock layers, there seemed to be a clear reason that we were finding only fragments of bone. The layers of rock around the *puesto* were composed primarily of cemented—that is, compressed and hardened—sand and gravel. Many layers contained pebbles and even small boulders. The sand and gravel had probably been deposited near the base of some hills by ancient rivers. Wedges of sand and gravel like this are called alluvial fans.

The bad news from our point of view was that fast currents are required to carry such large pebbles and boulders, and when fast currents carry large objects, most skeletons of dinosaurs and other animals swept along get badly broken. So, although these rock layers were beautiful, and sometimes contained small pockets of mud and silt that might preserve more complete fossil bones, they were

After prospecting in the rocks behind the *puesto* without finding much, we decided to look at sites farther away, like these badlands.

probably not the best place to look for well-preserved fossil skeletons.

However, from the top of these outcrops near the *puesto* we could see glowing reddish brown badlands off in the distance. Perhaps we might find better fossils there. It certainly seemed worth a try—that is, if we could find a way to get to them.

November 9. As we bounced toward the main road from Neuquén, we passed a gap in a small ridge, and through the gap we spied the badlands we had spotted the previous day. Fortunately, a small dirt road ran through the gap, so we bumped a mile or two down that road into the center of the sunlit layers of ancient rock.

After parking by the side of the road, the crew decided to prospect the area for an hour or two to see if we could find any clues that would lead us to new fossils. Most trips like this are unsuccessful, and we had no great expectations. But our dream of discovery was about to come true. Our field notes exclaim this was a "Big day!"

As we walked onto the flats adjacent to the beautifully banded layers of sandstone and mudstone, we kept our eyes glued to the ground, searching for scraps of fossil bone.

Within five minutes crew members began kneeling down to examine dark gray fragments of rounded rock. Picking these chunks up for closer inspection, we noticed that the surface of these rounded rocks was sculpted with curious small bumps and depressions. We knew immediately from that distinctive texture that we had found something remarkable—dinosaur eggs. But what kind?

These particular eggs were large but not enormous as dinosaur eggs go—five to six inches across. Eggs this size and even larger had been found in Patagonia, as well as in other areas of the world. In fact, these were like the first dinosaur eggs ever found. Those first eggs were found in France,

The eggs we found were large—compare their size to the sizes of the rock hammer and paintbrush.

in rocks that had been deposited near the end of the Age of Large Dinosaurs. Paleontologists had always assumed, because of their large size, that they belonged to giant plant-eating sauropods. But we were not so sure, because no sauropod embryos had ever been found inside those eggs.

Fossils of embryos are very rare because they represent the fragile skeletons of baby dinosaurs that have not yet hatched. Such

Sauropod dinosaurs were the largest animals that ever walked the earth—much bigger than elephants (and humans).

small, delicate skeletons are hardly ever preserved; they either decay or are destroyed before they become fossilized. The lack of any embryos in these eggs concerned us.

Still, we knew that sauropods had lived in this area near the end of the Age of Large Dinosaurs. We had found parts of their skeletons just the day before in the outcrops of cemented sandstone and gravel near the *puesto.* For decades paleontologists have recognized that sauropod dinosaurs represent the largest land animals ever known to have walked the earth. Their names roll off the tongues of children and adults alike: *Apatosaurus* (formerly known as *Brontosaurus*), *Diplodocus, Brachiosaurus,* and others. Adult remains of these animals have been collected on several continents; however, no skeletons of embryonic babies in their eggs had ever been found. So the ultimate clue needed to identify which dinosaur had laid the Patagonian eggs was still missing. Could we be the ones to find it?

The area over which the dinosaur eggs were exposed turned out to be immense. Acres and acres of reddish brown mudstone were exposed, and every few steps, a cluster of broken eggs sat on the surface. There were eggs everywhere, tens of thousands of them. It was hard to believe, because dinosaur eggs are very fragile, just like eggs you buy in the store. How could so many have survived for more than 70 million years? We were very excited, because we figured that a few of these eggs *had* to have embryonic bones preserved inside.

Soon one of the crew members approached us. He had found an egg with a small rocky sheet of bumpy material preserved inside. He thought the texture on the surface resembled dinosaur skin. But fossils of dinosaur skin and other types of soft tissue are extremely rare. Besides, no one had ever discovered fossils of embryonic dinosaur skin inside an egg, and the patch of textured rock was very small. Per-

Looking for fossils in the field often means getting down on your hands and knees. One of our crew members, Carl Mehling, sits by a cluster of fossil eggs, looking for embryonic bones.

haps it was just some unusual mineral crystals. To be certain that it was skin, we would have to find more.

By the end of the day we were tired but thrilled. We knew we had discovered a remarkable new fossil site, though we were

still not sure exactly what kind of dinosaur eggs we had found.

Eggs Everywhere

November 10. In the morning we returned to our new site. Most of us continued searching for dinosaur eggs, hoping to find more fossils of the possible embryonic skin and maybe even some bones. As our field notes say, "The layer with eggs goes on forever. There must be many thousands of nests spread over several square miles. But all the eggs seem to be restricted to a single layer of rock."

A few of us tried to estimate how many eggs and nests were exposed in a small portion of the flats. We tied colored tape to the branches of small bushes to mark out a trapezoid. This area was staked out using a small hand-held computer called a Global Positioning System (GPS). Using signals from satellites orbiting Earth, the GPS unit calculates the latitude and longitude of the point where you're standing. With this information, we could calculate

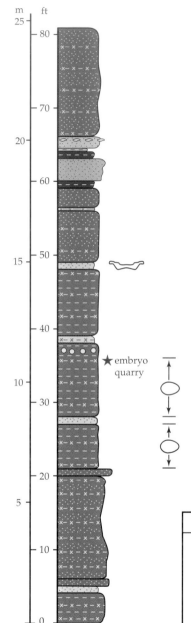

★embryo quarry

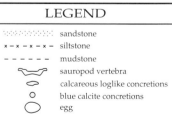

Some crew members began studying the rocks that contained the fossils. The most important geological job was to start at the bottom of the rock layers and measure how thick each layer of sandstone and mudstone was. As we took the measurements, we drew in our field notebook a picture of the different rock layers. This picture is called a strati-graphic section. The drawing is important for telling time because layers of rock are laid down one on top of the other. The lowest layer is the oldest, and the highest layer is the most recent. It's critical to record which layer or layers contain the fossils, because fossils from lower layers lived earlier than fossils from higher layers.

LEGEND	
⋯⋯⋯⋯	sandstone
x – x – x – x –	siltstone
– – – – –	mudstone
⌣	sauropod vertebra
⬯	calcareous loglike concretions
○	blue calcite concretions
⬭	egg

the length of each side of our trapezoid. The two sides were each approximately 1,000 feet long, with the top about 250 feet across and the base around 400 feet across. Within that area we counted 195 clusters of eggs.

The abundance of eggs triggered a discussion about what we should name our new fossil site. After brainstorming, we agreed on what we all thought was the best name—Auca Mahuevo. The name is a pun on the local region's name, Auca Mahuida, but it also refers to the seemingly countless eggs preserved at the site. *Mahuevo* is a shortened combination of two Spanish words, *más huevos*, which means "more eggs."

The dinosaurs at Auca Mahuevo lived during the last period of the Mesozoic Era, the Cretaceous Period. It lasted from 145

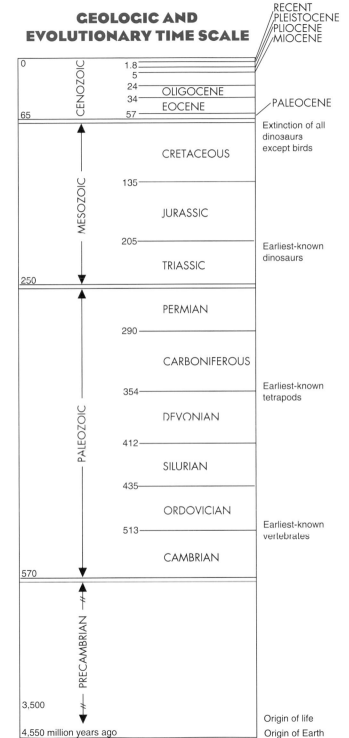

GEOLOGIC AND EVOLUTIONARY TIME SCALE

RECENT		
PLEISTOCENE		
PLIOCENE		
MIOCENE		
0 — CENOZOIC	1.8	
	5	
	24 — OLIGOCENE	
	34	
	EOCENE — PALEOCENE	
65 —	57	
		Extinction of all dinosaurs except birds
MESOZOIC	CRETACEOUS	
	135	
	JURASSIC	
	205	Earliest-known dinosaurs
250 —	TRIASSIC	
PALEOZOIC	PERMIAN	
	290	
	CARBONIFEROUS	
	354	Earliest-known tetrapods
	DEVONIAN	
	412	
	SILURIAN	
	435	
	ORDOVICIAN	Earliest-known vertebrates
	513	
	CAMBRIAN	
570 —		
PRECAMBRIAN		
3,500 —		
4,550 million years ago		Origin of life — Origin of Earth

Because ancient animals and plants lived so long ago, geologists and paleontologists have had to develop a special kind of calendar to measure and understand these long-past periods of Earth's history. The calendar is called the geologic time scale. Based on major changes in the kinds of fossil animals and plants that lived at different times during the history of Earth, this calendar is divided into four major eras. From longest ago to most recent, they are the Precambrian (4.5 billion to 600 million years ago), the Paleozoic (600 million to 250 million years ago), the Mesozoic (250 million to 65 million years ago), and the era we now live in, the Cenozoic (65 million years ago to the present). The Mesozoic Era, sometimes called the Age of Large Dinosaurs, is divided into three different periods. The earliest is the Triassic Period, which lasted from 250 million years ago until about 205 million years ago. The earliest known dinosaurs lived in the Triassic, about 228 million years ago. Next comes the Jurassic Period, which lasted from 205 million years ago to 145 million years ago. This is the period for which the movie **Jurassic Park** is named, although many of the dinosaurs featured in the film actually lived either before or after the Jurassic. The Jurassic saw the evolution of most of the largest dinosaurs that ever lived, such as **Apatosaurus** (formerly called **Brontosaurus**), **Diplodocus**, and **Brachiosaurus**.

Some rocks in other parts of the world that contain fossils similar to the ones we found in Patagonia also contain ancient layers of weathered volcanic ash, like the huge clouds of dusty ash that erupted out of Mount Saint Helens in 1980. The volcanic ash contains small crystals of minerals that were formed just before the volcano erupted. These crystals are made up, in part, of atoms that break apart into other atoms at a constant rate. The atoms that break apart are called parent atoms, and the atoms that the parent atoms break apart into are called daughter atoms. The process of breaking up is called radioactive decay.

Using special instruments, we can estimate how long it takes for half of the parent atoms to break up into their daughter atoms. We can also measure how many parent and daughter atoms are present in the small crystals that were formed just before the volcano erupted. When we know these amounts, we can calculate the age of the layer of volcanic ash and find out approximately how old the fossils in the nearby rock layers are.

million years ago until 65 million years ago. Figuring out exactly how old the fossils from Auca Mahuevo are is difficult and involves detailed scientific detective work. One method we use is to compare animals at Auca Mahuevo with fossil animals of known age from other places. If they're very similar, then we can assume that the fossils from Auca Mahuevo are about the same age. Using just the dinosaurs, it's very hard to tell. However, there are some fossils of animals in nearby rock layers that lived in the ocean, such as clams, snails, and microscopic plankton. These suggest that the dinosaurs at Auca Mahuevo are between 89 and 71 million years old.

We hoped to find another clue to how old these fossils were in the greenish sands at Auca Mahuevo. If they contained min-

Collecting rock samples, as Lowell Dingus is doing here, is an important task. We hope to learn how long ago our fossils lived by figuring out how old the rocks surrounding them are.

erals that had erupted out of volcanoes, we might be able to date them radioactively. We collected many samples of the greenish sands for analysis back in the laboratory.

But in the meantime we looked for other clues in the rock layers about what kind of environment the dinosaurs lived in. It became clear immediately from looking at the rocks that the dinosaurs lived on an ancient floodplain. This floodplain formed as South America drifted away from Africa, pushed by the enormous forces generated deep within the earth as part of a geologic process called plate tectonics. Thin layers of sandstone told us that in ancient times, shallow stream channels had crossed the floodplain. The eggs themselves, however, were confined to finer-grained muds and silts that were deposited during floods when the streams overflowed their banks. It appeared that the dinosaurs looked for places away from the streams in safer areas of the floodplain to lay their eggs.

As we continued to work, we had more success finding fossils. We had discovered two eggs of great importance. Both contained fragments of embryonic bones. The fragments were still not large enough to allow us to identify what kind of dinosaur had laid the eggs, but they told us that if we kept looking we might find ones that did. As our field notes say, we were already suspecting that the "Place will probably go 'big time.'"

The first fossils of embryonic dinosaur skin ever discovered.

Fossil Dinosaur Skin

November 11. The notes for this day begin with the statement, "Another day to remember." It was hard work, though. We examined thousands of fossilized egg fragments strewn across the surface of the flats and adjacent ravines, looking for embryonic bones. Most of the fragments contained no embryonic remains. However, one contained a large patch of mineralized bumps, like the small

After an exciting day in the field, Julia Clarke and Luis Chiappe celebrate with a big barbecue.

patch we had found during our first day at the site. This new, large patch was ornamented with scaly-looking bumps crossed by a triple row of larger and more rectangular plates. When we looked at this egg, we had no doubt: We had discovered the first fossils of embryonic dinosaur skin ever found. Members of the crew hugged each other, sharing the thrill of our success.

Although we were overjoyed with our good fortune, it took a while for the significance of the discovery to really sink in. Fossilized skin is very rare because the skin quickly decays after the animal dies. But it's the only direct evidence we have of what dinosaurs actually looked like when they were alive. Furthermore, very little is known about dinosaur embryos. So we had found an important missing piece of the scientific puzzle that needed to be put together for us to fully understand these long-extinct animals—what they looked like when they were first born. Amazingly, the skin of the embryos that our crew found was not merely an impression left by the skin in the surrounding mud. Our specimens were three-dimensional fossilized reproductions of the *actual* skin of the embryo.

On the other side of the flats, our geologic work continued. Besides collecting rock samples for possible dating by measuring radioactivity, we collected rock samples for magnetic analysis. These samples might also contain clues that could help us estimate how old the rocks containing the eggs were.

We had been in the field only four days, but we already knew that our expedition had succeeded beyond our wildest dreams. As we drove back to camp at the end of the day, we were very pleased, but we also knew our job wasn't finished. We had to find more embry-

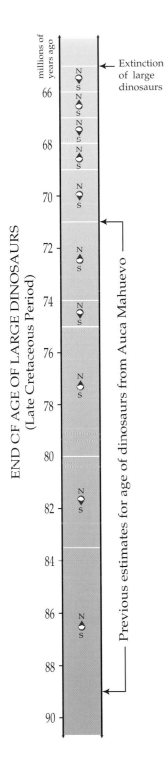

millions of years ago

← Extinction of large dinosaurs

66

68

70

72

74

76

78

80

82

84

86

88

90

END OF AGE OF LARGE DINOSAURS
(Late Cretaceous Period)

Previous estimates for age of dinosaurs from Auca Mahuevo

Magnetic Dating

Earth is like a giant bar magnet with a north pole and a south pole. Throughout the known history of Earth, the planet's magnetic poles have occasionally switched directions, so that the magnetic end of a compass needle that points north today would have pointed south. In the past 65 million years, the magnetic poles have switched positions about thirty times. The last time the poles switched positions was about 750,000 years ago.

If we collect samples of rock from the layers containing the fossilized eggs, we can estimate the age of the rocks by finding out whether or not they were formed when the poles were oriented the way they are today. So we collected rock samples from eight different layers associated with the fossil eggs. The magnetic measurements would determine whether the rocks had been formed during a "normal" or "reversed" period in Earth's magnetic history.

LEGEND

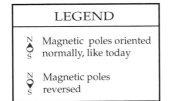

N♢S Magnetic poles oriented normally, like today

N♢S Magnetic poles reversed

onic bones that would help us identify for sure what kind of dinosaur had laid the eggs. But tonight we would celebrate our success with a tasty *asado* featuring beef and goat, and dancing.

The First Embryo

November 12. We resumed our search for embryos, but with a slightly different strategy. Up to this point, we had been concentrating on the eggs exposed on the flats adjacent to the ridges in the badlands. But on this day we decided to focus our search on the badland ridges and ravines themselves. At a spot about a half mile from the flats, two crew members found a hillside below a ridge littered with eggshell fragments. Quarrying in under the surface of the reddish brown mudstone, they discovered many complete, well-preserved eggs. As they began to dig into one of the eggs, small, thin, brown bones appeared. Our quest to find an embryo had finally succeeded!

The bones appeared to fit up against one another, and their shape suggested that they

23

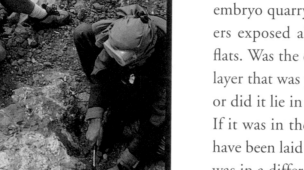

when we got them back to the laboratory in the museum and prepared them properly.

In terms of geological work, our biggest job was to make sure we knew where the new embryo quarry fit in the sequence of rock layers exposed along the ridges and across the flats. Was the embryo quarry in the same rock layer that was producing eggs back at the flats, or did it lie in a different egg-producing layer? If it was in the same layer, all the eggs would have been laid at about the same time. But if it was in a different layer, the site would contain two nesting grounds that had been inhabited at distinctly different times.

As geologic detectives, how did we solve this mystery? We walked on the egg-producing layer all the way from the quarry back to the flats. We traced the layer that contained the eggs across the rugged ridges and ravines of the badlands back to the area around the flats where we had measured the stratigraphic section. It turned out that the quarry was in the same layer of mudstone that had produced fossilized eggs on the flats. Auca Mahuevo contained just one enormous nesting site.

formed the leg of a baby dinosaur. Each one was only three or four inches long, but that's actually rather large for embryonic bones. Although we could not identify them for sure in the field, we were pretty certain we would be able to say which dinosaur they came from

Collecting Eggs

November 13–27. The wind blew mercilessly throughout one night and the next day. We estimated that gusts as fast as fifty miles per hour stormed across the dusty landscape, sandblasting everything in their path, including our eyes. Many of our tents were blown over or damaged, so we had to spend much of the day tending to our camp.

Over the next two weeks, we collected dozens more eggs, both fragments of eggs with patches of fossilized skin from the flats, and clusters of eggs containing some bones of embryos from the quarry in the badlands. Sometimes, collecting the clusters of eggs required making large plaster jackets to protect the eggs during the trip back to the museum. Some of the plastered blocks of mudstone contained more than twenty eggs and weighed several hundred pounds. These were pretty difficult to move, even with a lot of people helping to pull and lift. As is often the case, we couldn't drive our truck all the

way to the place where the eggs had been found.

To get the heavy blocks down the hill to the truck, we borrowed a large sheet of scrap metal from Doña Dora. After we'd punched holes at each corner of the sheet with our rock hammers and attached ropes, we had a sort of sled on which we could load the blocks and slide them down the hill. Some crew members pulled on the ropes in front, while others steadied the block and the sled with the ropes attached to the back. Still, it took almost all

Some of the plaster jackets containing clusters of fossil eggs were too heavy to lift, and the terrain was too rugged to drive to them, so we had to drag them to the truck on a homemade sled.

Our campsite at the *puesto* was home during the weeks we were in Patagonia.

our crew to move the blocks about fifty yards from the quarry down the hill to the trucks. And lifting them into the back of the pickup was no easy task either. But with everyone helping, we managed to get the job done.

We also collected more rock samples in hopes that they might contain fossilized microscopic pollen. The pollen would give us clues about the kinds of plants that lived on or near the floodplain where the dinosaurs laid their eggs. However, such analyses would once again have to wait until we got the samples back to the laboratory.

We spent a few more days looking at exposures of rocks in the region around Auca Mahuida, as well as prospecting for fossils in rock layers around the city of Neuquén.

The rocks throughout the area were spectacularly beautiful. Some exposures were ominously overseen by large vultures and condors soaring high above us. During one of these prospecting side trips, our pickup truck broke down. We were about twenty miles from camp. Fortunately, Rodolfo had come along with us in his pickup, so all ten of us crammed ourselves into the cab and the back of his truck for the rough ride back.

The End of an Adventure

November 27. We broke camp and began the two-day drive to Buenos Aires. It had been the adventure of a lifetime, but the work that was needed to figure out exactly what we had found had just begun. We were eager to get all our fossils back to the museum. In the preparation lab, we could clean up the fossilized eggs and begin trying to solve the mystery of what kind of dinosaur had laid them.

Four

Who Laid the Eggs?

We arrived back in New York during the first week of December. Rodolfo and his museum in Plaza Huincul had allowed us to borrow several of the smaller fossils we had collected so that we could prepare them at the Peabody Museum on the campus of Yale University in New Haven and then study them at the American Museum of Natural History in New York. Rodolfo and his crew would prepare some of the larger blocks of eggs at the Carmen Funes Museum.

Preparing delicate fossils like our embryos requires a lot of skill and patience, as well as precision tools. Under a microscope, using a sharp steel needle, a preparator slowly and carefully picks away the rock surrounding the fragile bones. As the bones are uncovered, they are protected with thin coats of transparent glue. To prepare just one tiny fossil embryo could require days or even weeks of painstaking work. But it was the only way to find out which dinosaur had laid the eggs.

It wasn't until early January that news came from our preparator at Yale. She had made an important discovery. Inside one of

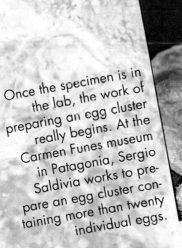

Once the specimen is in the lab, the work of preparing an egg cluster really begins. At the Carmen Funes museum in Patagonia, Sergio Saldivia works to prepare an egg cluster containing more than twenty individual eggs.

27

If you look carefully, you can see bones of a tiny dinosaur skull that was preserved inside this egg.

remains ever found of the tiniest giants.

Still, a great deal more research needed to be carried out. Most importantly, we needed to write a scientific paper to let other scientists know what we had found. As the preparation of the specimens continued throughout February, March, and April of 1998, we began to compile the research

the eggs, she'd uncovered miniature skull bones and microscopic teeth. The teeth, the skull bones, and the pattern of bumps on the fossilized skin gave us the clues we needed. The embryonic bones and teeth probably were those of a kind of sauropod dinosaur that belonged to the group called titanosaurs. Our ultimate dream for the trip had indeed come true. Our team had discovered the first

that would go into the paper. It would take us until early June to do the research and write a first draft. Then the paper would be sent off to a scientific journal. The staff of the journal would send our paper out to other paleontologists to get their comments and criticisms. This process is called peer review, and it's an important part of the scientific method. Once other scientists have made their comments, the editors at the journal decide whether the paper is important and accurate enough to publish. After a paper is accepted, it can still take well over a year for it to be published.

Clues in the Eggs

Compared to a chicken egg, a sauropod egg is huge, so you might not suspect that the animals that laid them are related.

Dinosaur eggs come in all shapes and sizes: round like a softball, oval like a football, large like an ostrich egg, and tiny like a humming-bird egg. You might be interested to know that both hummingbird and ostrich eggs are actually dinosaur eggs. This is because birds evolved from some small meat-eating dinosaur that probably looked a lot like *Velociraptor,* even though it lived much earlier than *Velociraptor.* And because birds descend-ed from a dinosaur, they are dinosaurs.

Dinosaur eggs are classified on the basis of their size, the pattern on the eggshell's surface, the microscopic structure of the crystals that make up the eggshell, and the pattern of air holes penetrating the eggshell. Our Patagon-ian eggs are round and relatively large, about the size of a softball. The eggshell, however, is rather thin, roughly a tenth of an inch thick. This may seem thick in relation to a chicken's eggshell, but it's much thinner than other dinosaur eggshells.

The surface of the kind of eggshell we found often has ridges shaped like small worms, but the surface texture of our eggs does vary. Some have a mostly smooth surface with only a few knobs sticking out. Others have many distinct knobs, and they are also somewhat thicker. We know that as water

29

The eggs we found often had ridges or bumps that covered the surface of the shell. This is how they looked when we first found them on the ground.

differ a bit from each other, they're all the same kind of egg.

The microscopic structure of the eggs we collected was preserved well enough that we could be certain they were the kind of eggs usually believed to be sauropod eggs. In fact, we now believe that our eggs may represent a new species of fossil sauropod eggs. In scientific language, the prefix *oo* refers to eggs. So our new type of egg represents a new *oospecies*.

Our eggs were laid in large clusters, and it's sometimes hard to tell the end of one cluster from the beginning of the next. The eggs in each cluster were irregularly placed, and they were in two or three layers laid one on top of the other. In contrast, the eggs found in the nests of other dinosaurs are often laid in a spiral pattern or a radial pattern, like the spokes of a wheel.

seeps through the ground, it can partly dissolve the minerals that make up the eggshell and dramatically change the way the shell looks. Perhaps this happened to some of the eggs from Auca Mahuevo. In any case, we're certain that although the eggs we found there

Large eggs like the ones we found in Patagonia have often been identified as sauropods, and those from the end of the Cretaceous are usually thought to belong to titanosaurs. However, the bone evidence we needed to make a definite identification of which dinosaur our eggs belonged to was hidden inside the eggs.

Clues in the Bones

What clues in the bones inside our eggs might tell us whether they were sauropod eggs?

Very few dinosaur embryos have been found, and even though thousands of suspected sauropod eggs have been found in France, Spain, India, Argentina, China, and other parts of the world, no definitive embryos of sauropod dinosaurs had ever been found until our team's discovery. So it was impossible to be sure what kind of dinosaur these eggs belonged to. Some small fossils from young sauropods had been discovered before, and some paleontologists regarded

them as embryos. However, they were either too big to really be embryos, or they were not found inside an egg—the proof that the animal had not hatched. Since the bones our crew found were inside the eggs, there was no question that the dinosaur inside had not yet hatched.

Understanding the structure of these small fossils is never easy. Because the animals were so young, the delicate bones were not usually

Our embryo's skull has certain things in common with a *Diplodocus* skull (shown here), including the shape of the teeth.

well developed, and they were often crushed against the eggshell as the fluid in the egg was lost and the bones became fossilized. Unfortunately, our specimens are no exception.

Nonetheless, it's clear that one of our eggs holds a nearly complete skull, and another contains a less complete skull. These skulls contain very important clues for identifying the kind of dinosaur that laid the eggs because the skulls of different kinds of dinosaurs are usually quite distinctive. Our tiny dinosaur skulls are also remarkable because few adult sauropod skulls have been discovered, let alone embryo skulls. There were enough complete bones in the skulls of our embryos to allow us to make a fairly accurate reconstruction of what the skull looked like.

As with any other baby animal, the skull of our sauropod embryos was large in proportion to its body, though the whole head was only about two inches long. Likewise, the eye socket in our embryos was probably slightly larger in relation to the rest of the

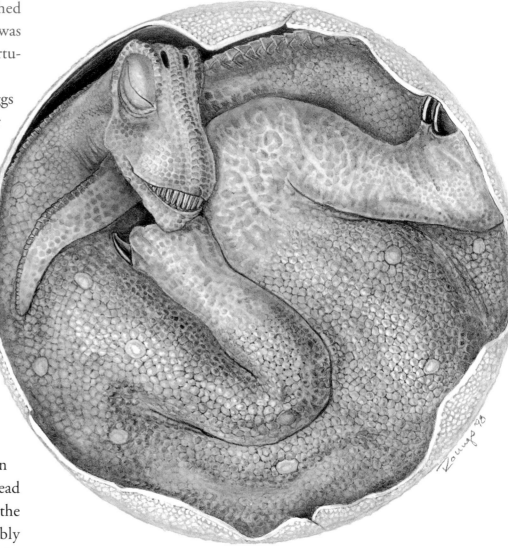

A baby titanosaur inside its egg may have looked like this.

SEMs

An electron micro-scope can magnify an object tens of thou-sands of times. The pho-tographs taken by the electron microscope are called SEMs, short for scanning electron micrographs. At the American Museum of Natural History, we have an SEM machine that requires that the speci-mens be coated with a thin layer of gold before images can be taken. We did not want to coat our real specimens because we wanted to preserve their original surface. Ironically, the fossils are much more valuable to scientists without a gold coating than with one. So we produced a rub-ber mold of our most complete patch of skin, and from that mold we made a resin cast of the skin. This perfectly repli-cated patch of embryon-ic dinosaur skin was coated with a very thin layer of gold and then photographed. Luckily, we also had the chance to obtain images of the embryonic skin using a more sophisticated elec-tron microscope. In this case, we did not have to make a cast of the speci-men, since the newer machine did not require a gold coating.

skull than the eye socket in adult sauropods.

Our embryos had tiny, pencil-shaped teeth in both the upper and lower jaws. The crown, or upper surface, of these teeth was formed by enamel, the same very durable material that forms the crowns of your teeth, as well as those of many other animals. The shape of the embryos' teeth is similar to that of *Diplodocus*, the famous whip-tailed sauropod from the Late Jurassic of the American West. Some of the cheekbones of our embryos are also shaped like those of *Diplodocus*.

Another of our eggs contained several leg bones that fit up against one another. The thigh bone is almost four inches long, indicat-ing that, when it hatched, this baby would have been twelve to fourteen inches long.

Clues in the Skin

The pattern on the skin of our babies looks very similar to that of other sauropod dinosaurs, such as *Diplodocus*. Recent discov-eries have shown that these Late Jurassic sauropods had a row of narrow spines running

along their tails, like crocodiles. Some scien-tists argue that this series of spines would also have extended along the back and neck. None of the patches of fossilized skin that our crew found shows signs of spines on our embryos. However, we believe that the triple row of scales found on our babies did extend along the entire tail, back, and neck.

Although many of the small bones and teeth and much of the skin inside our eggs look like those of *Diplodocus*, our embryos come from rocks that do not contain fossils of *Diplodocus*. In fact, many of the sauropods

© N. FRANKFURT

Some sauro-pods may have had a row of spines running down their tails, as croco-diles do today.

33

A photograph of our embryonic dinosaur skin shows that it looks a lot like reptile skin.

Among the titanosaurs that are known from the Late Cretaceous rocks we were exploring near Auca Mahuida, the most abundant is *Neuquensaurus,* a close relative of another Late Cretaceous titanosaur from Argentina called *Saltasaurus.* The titanosaur *Saltasaurus* is well known because it was completely covered with bony armor imbedded in its skin, presumably for protection from the large meat-eating dinosaurs that lived at the time. The pattern of armor plating in the skin of *Saltasaurus* is remarkably similar to the pattern of bumps on the skin of our Patagonian babies.

Dinosaur soft tissues, such as muscles, skin, and feathers, are rarely preserved in fossils. Although fossils of adult sauropod skin have been known since the mid-1800s, our crew's discovery was the first to document the skin of baby sauropods that had not hatched yet. In fact, our eggs were the first of any embryonic dinosaur in which the skin had been preserved.

To study the skin of our embryos, we first wanted to take photographs using an electron microscope.

we're familiar with (for example, *Diplodocus, Apatosaurus, Brachiosaurus,* and *Camarasaurus*) became extinct long before the Late Cretaceous. Instead, the rocks our eggs came from contain fossils of other sauropod dinosaurs called titanosaurs. These dinosaurs are extremely common in South America, although they've also been found in southern North America, Europe, Africa, and Asia.

34

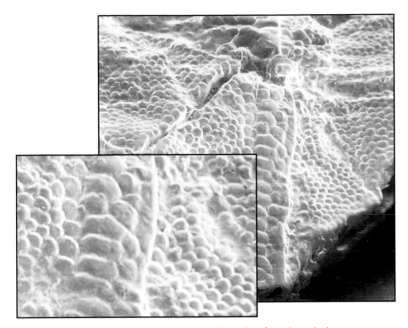

These SEMs let us take a close look at the fossilized skin.

Even at high levels of magnification, our embryonic dinosaur skin looks similar to the scaly skin of other reptiles to which dinosaurs are distantly related, like lizards. Basically, the skin is formed by a blanket of round, scalelike knobs of similar size. Occasionally a larger knob appears in the center of a rose-shaped pattern of smaller knobs, or the smaller knobs are crossed by a triple row of larger knobs. Folds in the skin indicate that it was not close-ly attached to the muscles and bones. The folds probably formed in the areas around the joints.

This pattern of scales is very similar to the clusters of bony plates called scutes that were discovered around the skeleton of *Saltasaurus*. The armor of *Saltasaurus* is formed by hundreds of small bony scutes, roughly the size of a human fingernail. The scutes are usually packed close together, but occasionally they're separated by larger oval scutes approximately four inches long. This combination of large and small scutes forms a roselike pattern like that found in our embryos. Both kinds of scutes are thought to have been embedded in the dinosaur's hide. However, the larger scutes of *Saltasaurus* have a high ridge that runs down the center. The larger scutes visible in the skin of our embryos do not show any type of central ridge. These scutes have a smooth surface, as shown in the SEMs.

How can we tell which group of sauropods our embryos belong to? Titanosaurs flourished in the Late Cretaceous, but they aren't the only group of Late Cretaceous sauropods.

Some poorly known skeletons indicate that other kinds of sauropods lived about the same time. This make it difficult to identify the specific group of sauropods to which the embryos from Auca Mahuevo belong.

The shape of the teeth and the roselike pattern of armor in the skin of our embryos is very similar to the teeth and pattern of bony armor found in the titanosaur sauropods. At this point, we can be certain that our embryos are sauropods, but we can't know whether our embryos really represent titanosaur sauropods or belong to some other group of sauropods until more complete embryos have been unearthed.

Clues About Reproduction

When paleontologists started studying sauropod dinosaurs, the sauropods' gigantic size made the scientists think that these animals gave birth to live young. For many paleontologists, it was hard to imagine how these enormous creatures could have laid eggs without crushing them. Even though paleontolo-

Dinosaur trackways often provide important clues about how dinosaurs lived.

gists discovered many large fossil eggs that were thought to have been laid by sauropods, this was just an educated guess, because no embryo of a sauropod had been found inside an egg. With our crew's discovery, we can be sure that at least one group of sauropods managed to lay their eggs without crushing them.

So now we know for sure that some sauropods laid eggs. We also know that they laid them in enormous colonies such as the one we found in Patagonia. Evidence from fossilized footprints and bone beds (collections of bones from a single dinosaur species in a single rock layer) indicates that sauropod dinosaurs were gregarious, meaning that they lived in groups. Herds of dozens of dinosaurs have been documented by large sequences of fossilized footprints. For example, in the 1930s a trackway of fossilized footprints representing twenty adult individuals was found in Bandera County, Texas. These discoveries paint a picture of the way these dinosaurs reproduced and lived that fits well with our discoveries in Argentina.

Pablo Puerta marks eggs with green paint to help us determine how many eggs are in a cluster.

Even though sauropods are known to have lived in groups and may have communicated with one another in some way, we still don't know whether the adults fed and protected their young. Parental care has been documented for other types of dinosaurs, including some meat-eating theropods. The first fossil dinosaur skeleton actually sitting on its nest of eggs was discovered in the Gobi Desert of

37

Mongolia. This provided solid evidence that certain types of dinosaurs, including *Oviraptor*, did care for their young. Evidence from other nesting grounds in Montana has suggested the same thing. The meat-eating dinosaur *Troodon*, one of the closest relatives of birds, has also been found to nest on top of its brood.

For the sauropods, however, the picture is not so clear. Some researchers believe that because the eggs were laid so close to one another, the huge size of the adults prevented them from taking care of the eggs. Furthermore, no hatchlings or juveniles have been found in the nesting grounds containing sauropod eggs. This evidence suggests that as soon as the sauropod embryos hatched, they left the nesting area and moved to feeding grounds. Although we have found many embryos at Auca Mahuevo, we have not found any hatchlings or juveniles in the same rock layer with the eggs. If this is really what was happening at the nesting site, and not a misleading problem with the way the fossils were preserved, it may mean that sauropods did not care for their young.

Clues in the Rocks

Unfortunately, none of the rock samples we brought back from the layers of greenish sandstone surrounding the fossil eggs contained mineral crystals that had erupted out of volcanoes. So unless we find samples on another trip that contain these crystals, we will not be able to estimate the age of the rock layers and eggs through the process of radioactive decay. Sometimes our attempts to learn about when dinosaurs lived fail. This is just a frustrating part of the job.

However, the rock samples we collected for magnetic analysis may be somewhat more helpful. The stratigraphic section containing the sauropod embryos at Auca Mahuevo may represent an ancient time interval when Earth's magnetic poles were reversed. If we can confirm that the rocks were formed when the magnetic poles were reversed, we will know that the rocks, eggs, and embryos from Auca Mahuevo are between 83 and 71 million years old. But more work is needed to be sure of this.

Five

The End of the Dream?

As often happens in paleontological research, what we discovered had little to do with our primary goal of finding fossil birds. Nonetheless, it turned out to be something no one had seen before. We discovered the first embryos of sauropod dinosaurs and the first dinosaur embryos ever found in South America. We also discovered the first embryonic dinosaur skin ever found anywhere. Looking back on our crew's adventure, it does seem somewhat like a dream—the months of anticipation leading up to the expedition, the days of exciting finds in the desolate badlands of Patagonia, and the months of careful detective work in the laboratory after the trip. The experience has been so intriguing that none of us wants it to end.

As we wrote our paper announcing the discovery of the fossils, we also began planning another expedition to Patagonia. Our goals for this trip will be a bit different than those for the last one. We'll spend more time prospecting and quarrying at Auca Mahuevo in hopes of finding skeletons of embryos that are even better preserved than the ones we've dug out so far. These could tell us whether or not the eggs were really laid by titanosaurs. We'll also continue to look for layers of altered volcanic ash with crystals that can be used to give us more precise estimates of when these dinosaurs lived. Best of all, we'll have the chance to explore new areas around Auca Mahuevo and fulfill our dreams of discovery once again. Maybe we'll even find some fossil birds next time.

About 80 million years ago, Patagonia looked very different from the way it looks today.

other experts on sauropods throughout the world.

Searching for clues in the shapes and structures of the embryos' bones might also help solve other mysteries. Although dinosaur embryos are extremely rare, they constitute the only evidence of the development and early rates of growth of dinosaurs. The study of dinosaur embryos could help us determine whether these creatures were warm-blooded or cold-blooded, and whether they took care of their young.

The list of mysteries goes on and on. All these mysteries will not be solved in the next few weeks or the next few months. Some might be, but not all. To solve them all will require years of hard detective work and dramatic discoveries by hundreds of paleontologists.

We can't wait.

But just working with what we've already found, we know we need to do a lot more, detailed scientific research to figure out how the different groups of sauropods are related to one another. The shapes of the bones of our embryos may prove extremely important in this work, which will involve not only our crew of paleontologists but also a number of

Glossary

armored dinosaurs dinosaurs such as ankylosaurs and stegosaurs whose bodies were protected by bony plates.

badland *or* **badlands** a geographic region marked by erosion, scarce vegetation, rugged ravines, and hills.

cast a replica or reproduction of a fossil made of fiberglass or plastic.

Cretaceous Period the final part of the Mesozoic Era (see time scale, page 19).

deposit the layers of mud, sand, and pebbles that have accumulated in an area after being carried there by water and wind.

Diplodocus a sauropod dinosaur with a small head, peglike teeth, a long, slim neck, and a tail that was carried aloft and ended in a whiplash tip.

embryo an animal at any stage of development before birth or hatching.

excavation the process of removing a fossil from the ground by digging.

fossil any trace of an ancient organism; usually the remains or impression of an animal or plant that has turned to stone. Skin and soft tissues rarely become fossilized; bones and teeth more commonly do.

geology the study of rocks, minerals, and fossils and the processes that form them.

impression a print made on the ground or on a rock by something pressed against it.

Jurassic Period the middle part of the Mesozoic Era (see time scale, page 19).

Mesozoic Era also called the Age of Dinosaurs; composed of three periods: the Triassic, Jurassic, and Cretaceous (see time scale, page 19).

microstructure the microscopic structure of the mineral crystals that make up a fossil.

paleontologist a scientist who studies ancient life and its fossil remains.

prospecting looking for fossils exposed on the surface of the ground.

quarrying excavating fossils from a large pit in a fossil-rich layer of rock.

Saltasaurus a sauropod dinosaur covered with body armor, or scutes.

sauropods giant, plant-eating dinosaurs that walked on four legs; noted for their long necks and tails and their relatively small heads.

scute a bony plate in the skin that helped to provide protection from predators.

stratigraphic section a drawing of rock layers in an area that describes their composition and thickness, as well as how they lie one on top of the other.

titanosaurs a group of plant-eating sauropod dinosaurs noted for their long necks, slim tails, and peg-shaped teeth. Primarily found on the southern continents during the Late Jurassic and Late Cretaceous periods.

trackway a series of fossil footprints left by an individual animal.

Triassic Period the first part of the Mesozoic Era (see time scale, page 19).

For Further Reading

Chiappe, L. M. "Dinosaur Embryos: Unscrambling the Past of Patagonia." *National Geographic*, December 1998.

Clark, J. "An Egg Thief Exonerated." *Natural History,* June 1995.

Currie, P. "The Great Dinosaur Egg Hunt." *National Geographic,* May 1996.

Horner, J., and J. Gorman. *Maia: A Dinosaur Grows Up*. Museum of the Rockies, Bozeman, Montana, 1985.

Norell, M., and L. Dingus, *A Nest of Dinosaurs: The Story of* Oviraptor. Doubleday Books for Young Readers, October 1999.

About the Authors

LOWELL DINGUS, Ph.D., directed the American Museum of Natural History's fossil hall renovation and served as head geologist on the museum's Gobi Desert expeditions, as well as many others.

LUIS CHIAPPE, Ph.D., is a research associate at the American Museum of Natural History and an adjunct professor at the City University of New York. He studies the evolution of early birds.